Traditional Witchcraft

Visualization

Simple exercises to develop your visualization skills

by Peter Paddon

Pendraig Publishing
Los Angeles, CA 91040
ISBN: 978-1936922802

Traditional Witchcraft: Visualization

First Edition

Copyright 2014 Peter Paddon
By Pendraig Publishing
All rights reserved

Cover Design & Interior Images, Typeset & Layout by: Peter Paddon

Pendraig Publishing
Los Angeles, CA 91040
ISBN: 978-1936922802

Table of Contents

Introduction

Anyone picking up a book on practical magick - or even many forms of spirituality that don't include magick - will sooner or later encounter visualization exercises. For some reason, this component of magical training is second only to trance for inducing fear in the heart of the student. Many people consider these simple components to be difficult, if not impossible.

I have been following my path for nearly forty years now, and for 25 of those years I have been teaching students. Over that period, I have encountered this fear in many students, and they genuinely appeared to have difficulty in achieving success in them. As a consequence, I have spent a lot of time working on exercises to overcome both the fear and the apparent difficulty, and have been quite successful in getting my students over this stumbling block which, coming as it does so early in their path, can frequently lead to disappointment with the path itself.

It seemed only fair to try to share the results of my experience further, which results in the book you hold in your hands. It is the first in a series of small, cheap books on basic subjects. I am aiming them primarily at students of Traditional Witchcraft, but to be honest, these are universal principles that are applicable to any magical path.

So, you might be asking yourself, what exactly is visualization anyway? It is a skill that, along with critical thinking, used to be much more common, but with the advent of movies, TV and the internet, has fallen into disuse. Sure, we still visualize, but it is a much more passive type of experience than it used to be, where we rely on the images provided, and look on passively at the creative efforts of others. In a simpler age, where entertainment was provided by books and radio, we had to engage much more actively, drawing on our imaginations to build a picture from the scenes and events described by the book or radio show. We are still visually oriented as a species, but modern humans, especially in developed countries, frequently forsake the active creation of our own imagery for the work of others.

In a nutshell, visualization is the ability to call up a visual representation of something that is not within our line of sight, or possibly doesn't exist in the mundane world. It is an act of imagination, and despite its name, frequently engages more than just the visual sense.

The next question that inevitably arises is this: why do we need it? As I mentioned above, we are visually oriented. What we see gets our attention much more effectively than what we hear, which is why radio dramas are much rarer than they used to be. As I will explain in more detail later in the book, one of the key components of successful spell-crafting is the ability to visualize the desired outcome of the spell, and it is also an important component of walking between the worlds and interacting with deities and other non-physical entities. It is possible to do all these things without visualizing, but it is far easier, and you get more consistent results, with visualization included in the mix.

There is hardly a magical technique that doesn't include visualization somewhere. Even something as simple as directing energy becomes much easier and potent when you visualize the energy in the form of colored light.

Pre-requisites

There are three simple requisites to successful visualization, and everyone possesses them to a greater or lesser extent. The first of these is imagination. One of the old axioms of magick – so old that nobody remembers who first said it – is that if you can imagine something, you can manifest it. The only limit to your abilities is your imagination. Magical practitioners power their spells by imagining the desired outcome, and artists, inventors and other creative folk imagine the finished result and work towards it. Michaelangelo famously described his sculpting technique as seeing the form trapped in the marble, and chiseling away all the stone that was not part of that form.

The second requirement is the ability to recall. Chances are, you can remember how to get home from your place of work, and while at home, you are able to recall and describe where you work. That is all this ability is – to be able to remember the journey or the appearance of the place or thing. It isn't something that we always consciously associate with visualization, but it is a key component of it. Recall is actually a powerful tool, and it is frequently triggered by the other senses; the smell

8

of a favorite dish can take you back to your childhood, when your mother or another relative cooked it for you, or a whiff of perfume causes you to recall a beautiful lover from many years ago. Listening to stories, poetry, and music can cause us to "recall" images and events that we have never experienced before, and that is where it begins to become a useful tool for magical studies.

The final pre-requisite is focus. Once again, modern entertainment has robbed many of us of the patience to pay attention, or focus, for longer than a moment. We jokingly refer to the "MTV Generation", where young people have an attention span that doesn't last longer than the average music video. As a result, focus is as misunderstood as visualization is by many students. We often think of focus in optical terms, using phrases like "laser-beam focus" and tunnel-vision" to describe it. When you are a scientist or engineer, that kind of focus is useful, but for the purposes of most magical operations, the sort of focus you are looking for is the kind once described as "single point focus". I like to refer to it as diffused focus, and it requires much less effort and concentration than the scientific "laser-like" focus. I'll be describing it in much more detail later.

Getting Started

Perhaps the most important thing when trying to develop visualization skills, is to identify exactly what visualization is. As I mentioned above, a large part of it is the ability to recall places, people and things we've seen before, and to imagine people, places and things we have never encountered in "real life". Visualization can be clear and detailed, as it is when we recall the face of a loved-one, our home, or a familiar object, but it can also be vague and "fuzzy", such as when we try to recall the face of someone we only met once, or a place we only know through photos and TV, or an object we've seen, but are unfamiliar with. Frequently, visualizations include non-visual information, such as texture, sound, scent and taste. Recalling the face of the one you love may also invoke the electric feel of their touch, the skipping of the heart, the fragrance of the shampoo they washed their hair with.

Visualization of stories, poems, etc., involves a combination of both familiar and strange items. We obviously have never visited Hogwart's School of Wizardry and Witchcraft (with the possible exception of a trip to Universal Studios in Florida), but we are familiar with castles, and schools, and the stereotypes of wizards and school kids, and so we combine these familiar components to extrapolate the image of the fictional school. Ultimately, even the recall of our lover's face turns out to be a combination of recall and imagination, as we tend to edit out the flaws in our lover's face, seeing them through the metaphorical "rose-tinted glasses".

There are several potential roadblocks to visualization, things that will get in the way of successfully recalling or imagining the desired images. First among these, and a demon that frequently rears its ugly head in many aspects of magical practice, is trying too hard and expecting too much. Another unfortunate influence of movies, TV and the internet in our lives is that we have come to expect glorious Technicolor and special effects by ILM. In reality, when you first actively pursue the skill of visualization, you are going to be very disappointed if you expect Hollywood-style effects. I made that mistake myself as a teenager, practicing my first pathworkings and visualization exercises. Instead of the bright colrs of the movie screen, what I got was colorless, vague, smoky and elusive. It was like expecting to see the 60" flatscreen TV that I have now, and instead getting the old black and white TV set (19-inch screen, no less) my father bought home when I was seven. I was deeply disappointed, and almost gave up, but I realized I was still getting results, and finally resigned myself to the idea that it was good enough, and carried on with my studies. It wasn't until much later, when I encountered the Lore of my Ancestors and connected viscerally to my magick, that the Technicolor imagery and all the rest became my normal experience.

Another roadblock, often connected closely to the first, is that people convince themselves that they "can't visualize" As we will see shortly, that is absolutely untrue, but it is surprisingly common. For example, I had a recent student share with me

"But I do have a problem with visualization. I have never been able see something in my mind eye after either closing my eyes or it has moved away. It doesn't matter if its human, animal, vegetable or mineral. I just can't recall what it look like. I know when I see it but just can't recall. I'm not sure what to do."

My response to her was this: The first thing to do is don't try too hard. You may be making assumptions about what visualization is. Look at an object, and then close your eyes. Don't try to "see" it, per se, just see if you can recall what it looks like. If you can, that is a good start. Stronger/clearer visualization comes with practice and patience, and not having expectations.

People often make the mistake of expecting visualization to look like actual seeing right off the bat. It can, with practice, but almost never does at first. Just allow yourself to be familiar with its appearance. If you can recall where something is that you left at home while you are away from the house, you have the ability to recall visual information, whether it looks like "seeing" or not. It may take a while to get to the point of good strong images - you may never get all the way there - but you have enough to work with for now, and it will improve with time and practice.

The other big roadblock is also kind of connected to the other two – having expectations that are too high. This is a common problem with many magical techniques, because too high an expectation can lead to self-imposed pressure. The pressure to succeed is quite capable of short-circuiting the whole process, as it often does in mundane endeavors. The trick here is to not make a big deal of it. When you are working on developing a skill of any sort, it is best to approach exercises as something you are doing to see what happens. Don't load yourself down with expectations – for a start, if you aim to high, you may completely miss a smaller success that doesn't "measure up" to your expectations, and more importantly, you are setting yourself up for failure, which can not only prove to be a self-fulfilling prophesy, but can make it harder to succeed the next time, because it knocks your confidence.

If you enter each exercise with more of a "let's see what happens" attitude, you don't have any expectations to meet, and therefore there is nowhere near the same amount of pressure. A a consequence, you are more likely to be aware of any improvement in your results, however slight, which will boost your confidence for next time.

Above all else, the biggest roadblock is expecting instant results. These things take time, because it is a bit like a physical ability – it is not enough to practice the ability, you have to "work out" to develop the mental/psychic "muscles" to be able to perform the thing you are trying to do. This is why in magick there are frequently exercises that apparently have nothing to do with the ability you are working on, but the build up your ability to do the things that your ability consists of. Even with the exercises directly concerned with the ability, it still takes time, there is rarely a "flicking of a switch" moment.

To counteract these roadblocks, there is one important fact that most people forget – we are all born with the ability to visualize, we just allow bad habits and laziness to take that ability away from us because in modern society it does not seem to be valued any more. There will be different levels of facility, and not everyone will be able to develop the ability to visualize in Technicolor, with all the special effects. But we can all at least get to the point where we can visualize well enough to be effective in our magical workings. As I told one student the other evening, you don't have to be the winner of the Tour de France in order to ride a bicycle to and from work.

One final point before we get into the practical work. A lot of new students make the assumption that you need a special place to practice these magical techniques – a quite space with subdued lighting and privacy, where you are unlikely to be disturbed. That is not so. Even if you are learning a meditation technique, I would suggest that you don't need to be more secluded or cocooned than for any other activity. Somebody who has only ever practiced a technique in a special place without distractions will find it very difficult to handle any distractions down the line. But if you learn to do your magick/meditation/spiritual exercise with ambient noise and other things going on around you, it might be a little harder at first, but you will benefit from never having to worry about distractions again.

For example, I first tried Tarot reading at a party, where there was loud music, drunken partiers (including me) and distracting nubile naked flesh. As I got into learning Tarot properly, I continued to do so in everyday places – a high street café, in my living room with people around and the TV on, and so on. As a result, I can read the cards at parties (I often get hired for Hollywood wrap parties, one of the erks of living in Los Angeles) without a problem. I have a friend who only ever practiced reading the cards in a meditational environment; she's very good, but can't read at parties to save her life.

Exercise 1: Recall

This exercise is aimed at breaking you in gently, as well as providing some context for those who believe they cannot visualize. It is a very simple exercise, which you should quickly succeed at.

Start by picking a familiar location that is not where you are right now. For example, if at home, you could pick where you work, or vice versa. Recall the place, and describe it. If you are alone, write down a description of it, or tell a partner what it looks like. Repeat this several times, each time trying to recall more detail. Keep going until you get to the point you start recalling things you weren't consciously aware of, then go and check to see if you were right. I can guarantee that by the time you reach this point, you will be actively visualizing the place. By the way, it doesn't matter if you are right or wrong about those final details – it is the act of recall that is important here.

When you feel comfortable and confident about your ability to recall the location, do the same exercise, but this time recall the journey from that location to where you are now, assuming you are familiar with that particular journey. Otherwise, recall a journey that you frequently make, and once again, each time try to recall more than you did the last time.

You can keep doing these two variants with different locations and journeys for as long as you feel the need, until you feel confident in your ability to recall. Then it is time for the next exercise.

Exercise 2: Imagination

Exercise two is pretty much the reverse f exercise one. Pick a passage from a story that describes a location in some detail, and have someone read it to you. If you are on your own, make an audio recording of you reading the passage, then use that for the exercise.

As you listen to the description, imagine how it looks. Try to visualize what is described. Once again, repeat this exercise multiple times (at least once per day), and each time, try to pick up on more details than before. After each read-though, share with your partner, or write down, the details about one feature of the description, each time aiming for more detail than the previous time. When you feel good about that passage, pick another from a different book, and repeat the exercise from the begin. Keep repeating the whole cycle until you feel confident in your ability to conjure up the location described in your mind's eye. Now, move on to the third exercise.

Exercise 3: Familiar Object Fly-by

This one is my favorite. Pick an everyday object, such as a ball-point pen, or a small ornament, or some other item you can easily hold in one hand. Start by observing the item, examining it closely in great detail, and familiarize yourself with every aspect of its appearance; the texture of its surface, the material any embellishments are made of, wear and tear on the item, and so on. Keep doing this for as long as it takes to become absolutely familiar with every detail of the object.

Once you reach that point, put the item away, close your eyes, and recall what the item looks like. "See" it in as much detail as you can, and each time you do so, try to get more detail, more realism into your visualization. Keep going until you get the image as clear and detailed as you can. Tis time, expand the size of the item, "zooming in" until it is enormous, big enough to be some weird space ship, and see yourself as an astronaut performing a fly-by prior to docking. In your mind's eye, fly around the object, making note of the familiar, but supersized, details. When you get good at this exercise, start again with a different object, and keep going until you are getting consistent results you can be confident about. Once you are able to do this, you should have no problem with visualization for the various magical techniques that require it.

Conclusion

It should hopefully be pretty obvious at this point that just like physical exercises, the secret is in repetition. In fact, I would recommend doing some variation of all three exercises at least once daily until you get the results you are after, and even after then, it doesn't hurt to revisit them from time to time, just to keep you at the level you want. Once you start being able to get consistent results in your ritual work, pathworkings and spellcrafting, then the confidence that brings will help you in other areas of your magick.

The benefits of developing skill in visualization don't stop with magical work, either. There are useful applications in the mundane world too. Visualization skills are excellent for creative work, such as painting, sculpting, costume design and other artistic pursuits, inventing and other problem-solving endeavors, even entertaining the kids with improvised storytelling.

The important thing to remember is that you do not need to achieve – or even aim for – perfection. There are some who have incredibly refined visualization skills, to the point that sometimes the people around them feel like they could see what the expert is visualizing. But that is a rare level of accomplishment, akin to a gold-medal Olympic skier. But we lesser mortals, though we might not have that gold medal, or that yellow jersey, or that Pulitzer Prize, can still ski, cycle, or write reports at a level that is competent, and useful for our needs. This is one occasion when "good enough" really is good enough.

Index